To —

Hope these bring
Thoughtful pleasure —

Jim Rhodes —
May - 29 - 86 -

The Lewiston Poetry Series

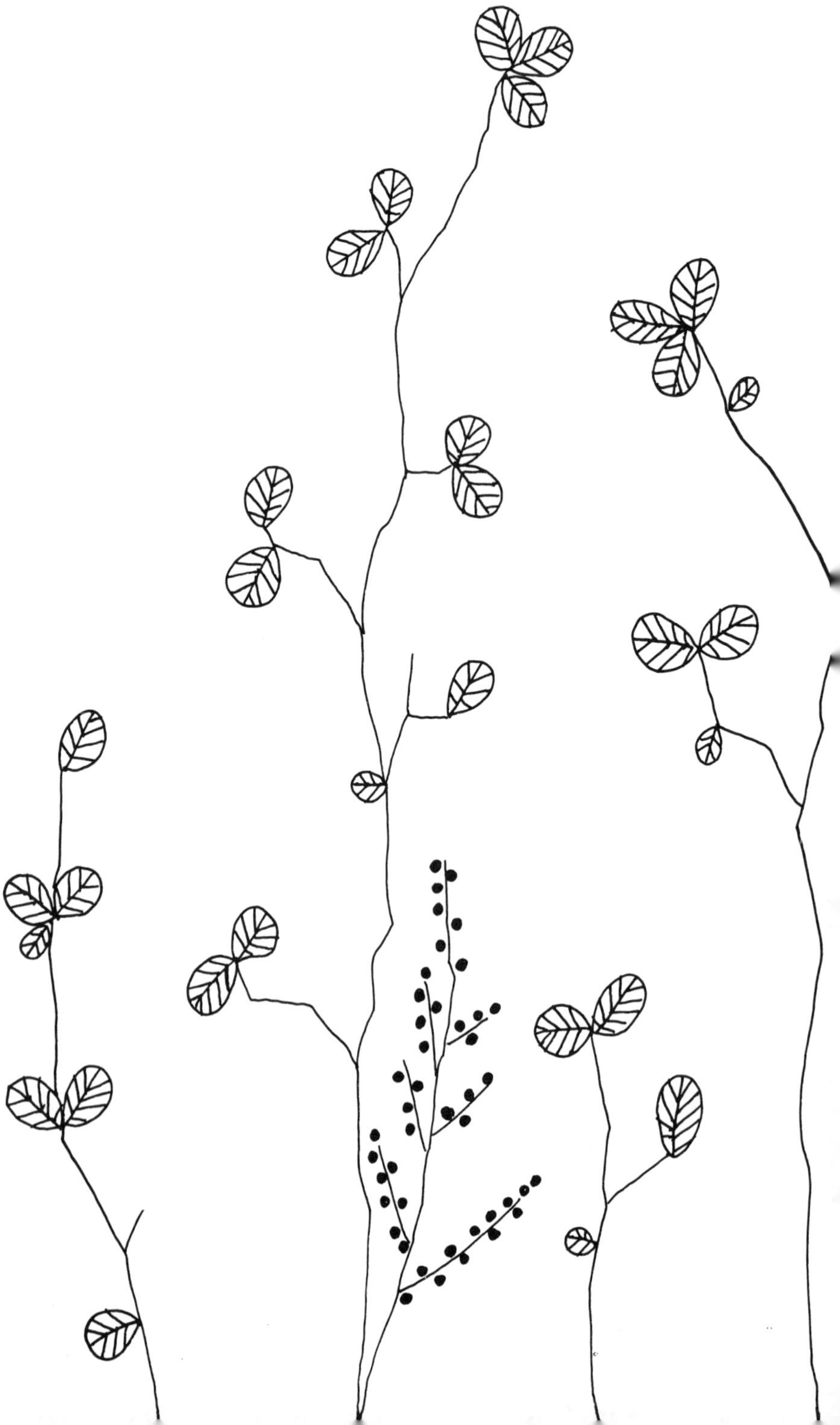

Little Vine

by James Rhodes
and Beth Kroecker

Little Vine

ISBN 0-88946-049-3

The Edwin Mellen Press
421 Center Street
Lewiston, New York 14092

© 1986 by James Rhodes

The poems in this book are by
James Rhodes.

The drawings are by
Beth Kroecker.

Beth Kroecker

When Hungry

I need
    Bread and butter,
But I love
    Honey on toast,
And what I love
    I need the most.

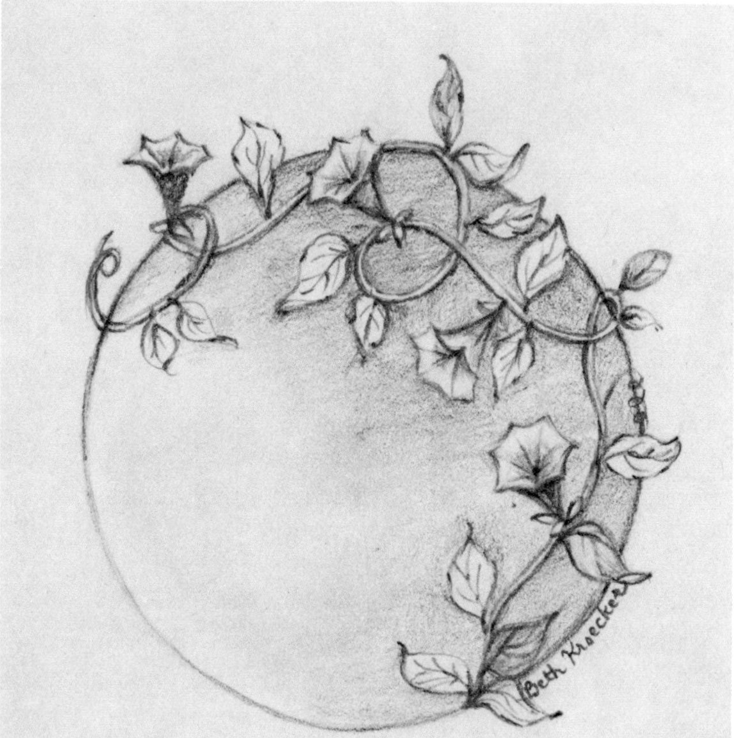
Beth Kroecker

Little Vine

Ah, little vine,
    I know you well;
I love your
    Twisting tendrils
Soft caress,
    Your clinging passion
Climbing the
    Twist in me;
Turning my growing
    To cover my death
With your greenness.

Beth Knoecken

Impossible Thought

What if
    Sunset and dawn
Should meet?
    If time
Should come
    Together
At the same place
    And cease?
Impossible thought
    At this late date;
But,
    Oh, what splendor,
Oh, what peace.

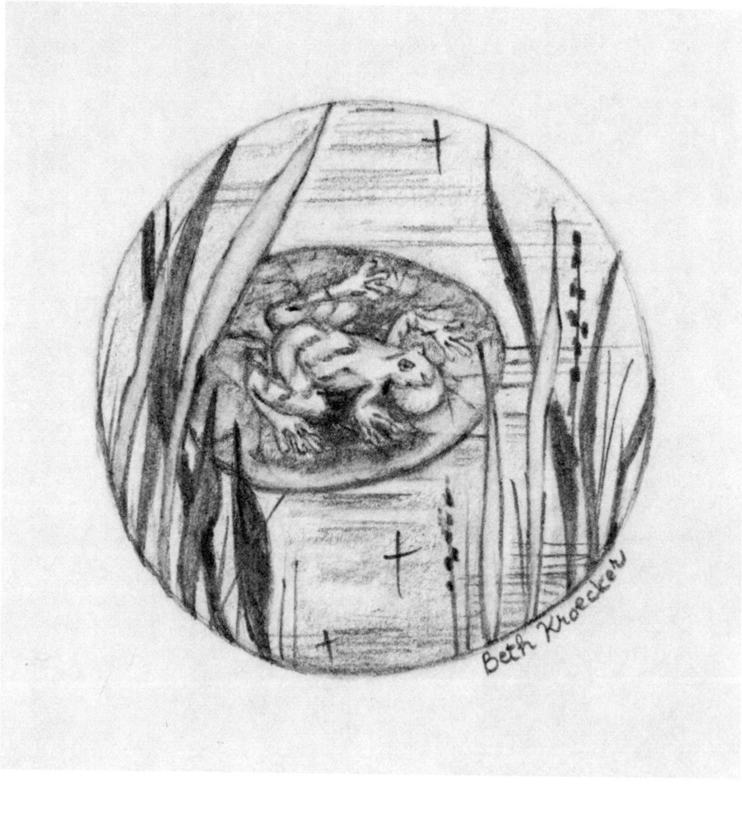
Beth Kroecker

Spring Magic

A thousand
    Piccolo peepers,
Five hundred
    Bass bull-frogs
Din the
    Starry night,
And sing the
    Misty bogs.

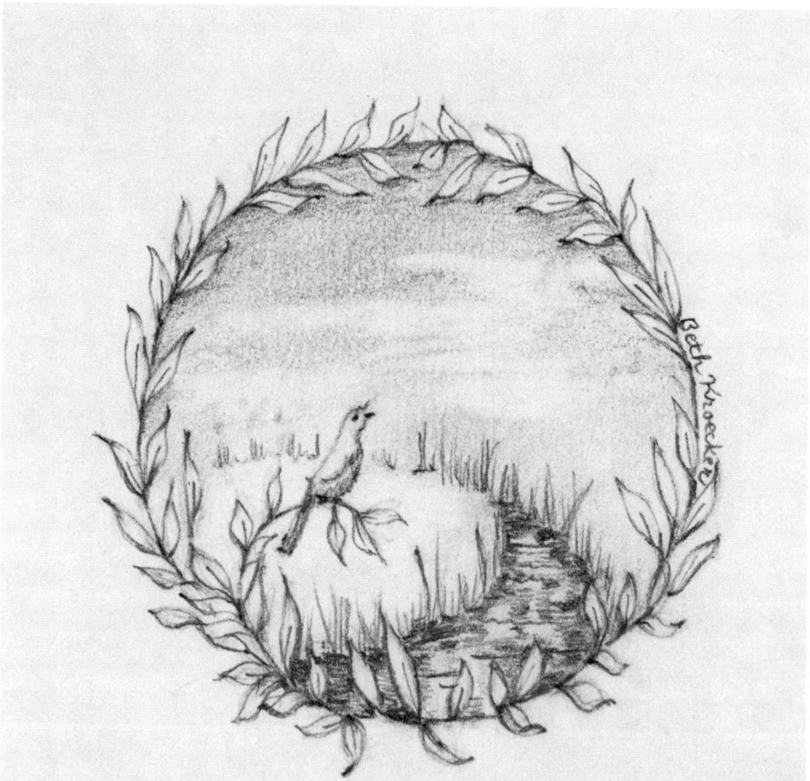
Beth Kroeker

Wing River

Today I watched
    A flow of wings,
Watched a river
    In the wind,
And heard
    A thousand
Starling sings.

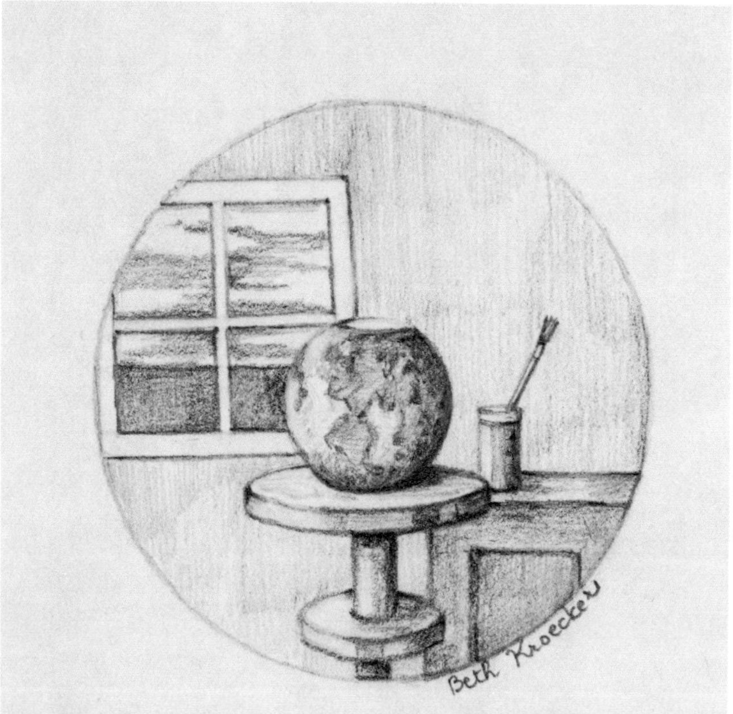
Beth Kroecker

Ceramic

Blue glaze
    Turns
Upon the wheels
    Of the Potters'
Earth and clays;
    While the Potters'
Wiping hands
    Finger tentative
Dawns and
    Sunsets
Across the
    Turning days.

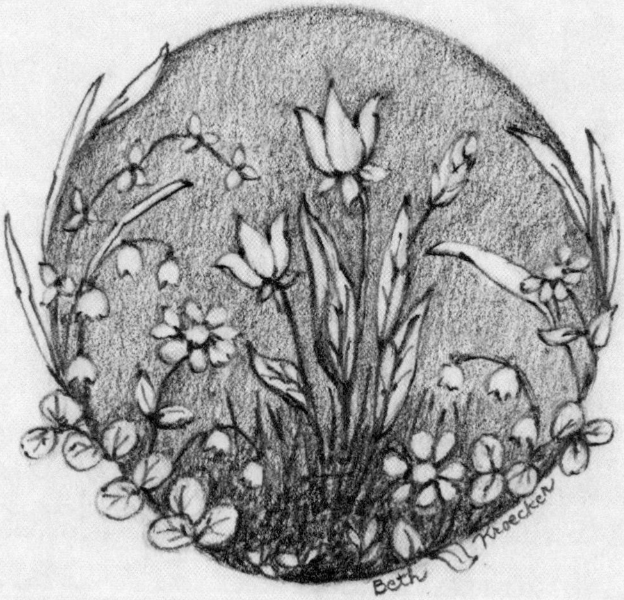
Beth Kroecker

Warmed

Do flowers
    Need a reason,
Excepting,
    Warmed
From earth
    In sunlight
Season
    They give
Answer
    Of themselves
And celebrate ?
    Neither
Do I.

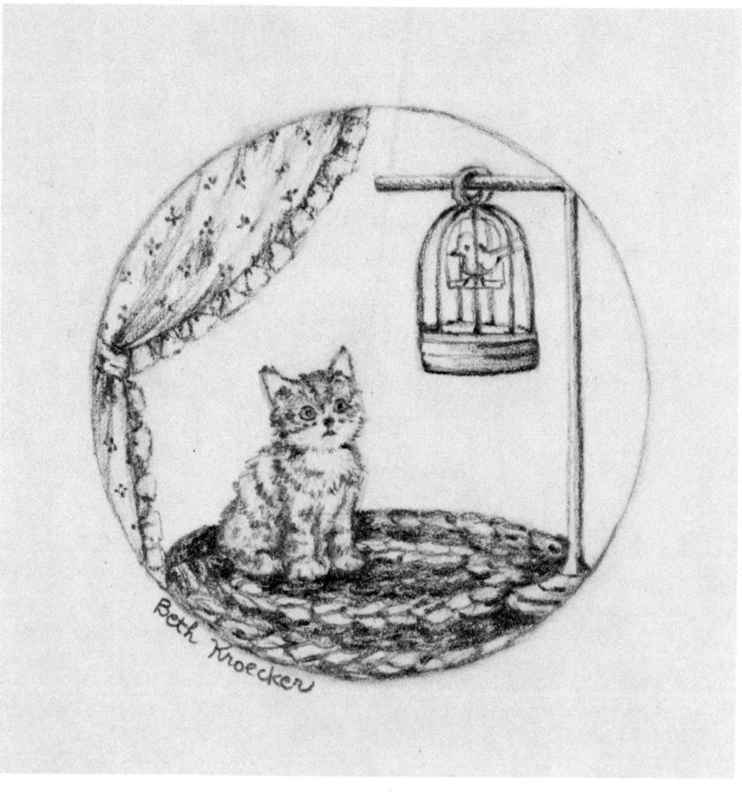
Beth Kroecker

Cat Song

Who loves
    Cats,
Remember;
    To a bird,
A cat
    Is wrong;
To a moth,
    Evil
Is a birdsong.

Beth Kroecker

You're Dead!

Tin soldiers,
     Toy guns,
Primitive appeal;
     War
Is boys
     Taught to play --
Gone real.

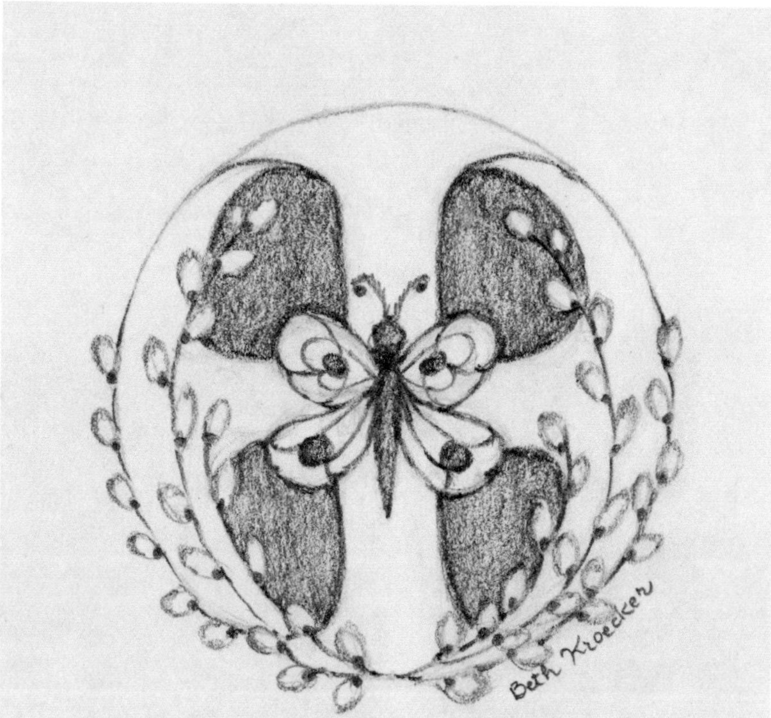
Beth Kroecker

Wings To Heaven

    If I could
Only understand
    The Butterfly;
Twice born
    And still being.

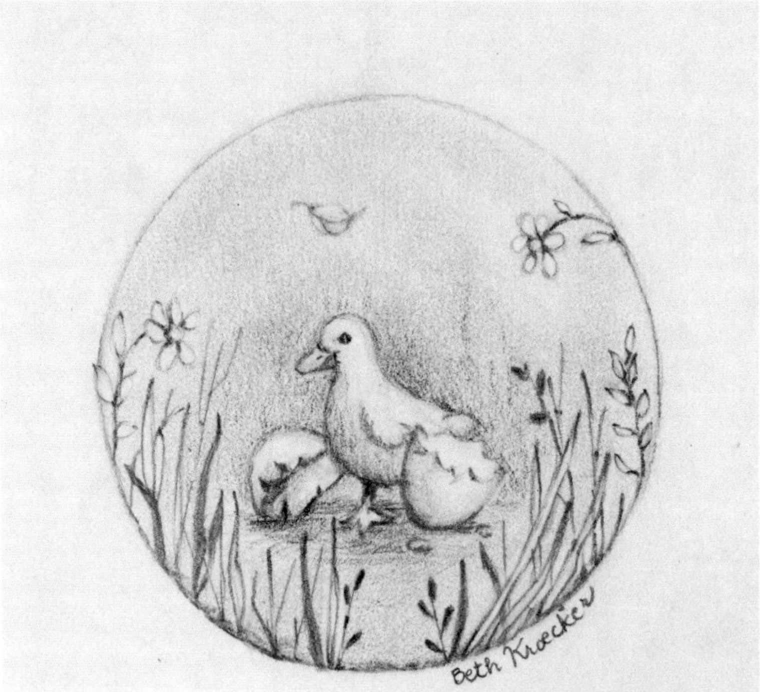
Beth Kroecker

Of Wings And Shells

Wings are for flying
    While shells are to hide in;
Dreams are for trying,
    With all life to be tried in;
The problem's not dying,
    But which one you die in.

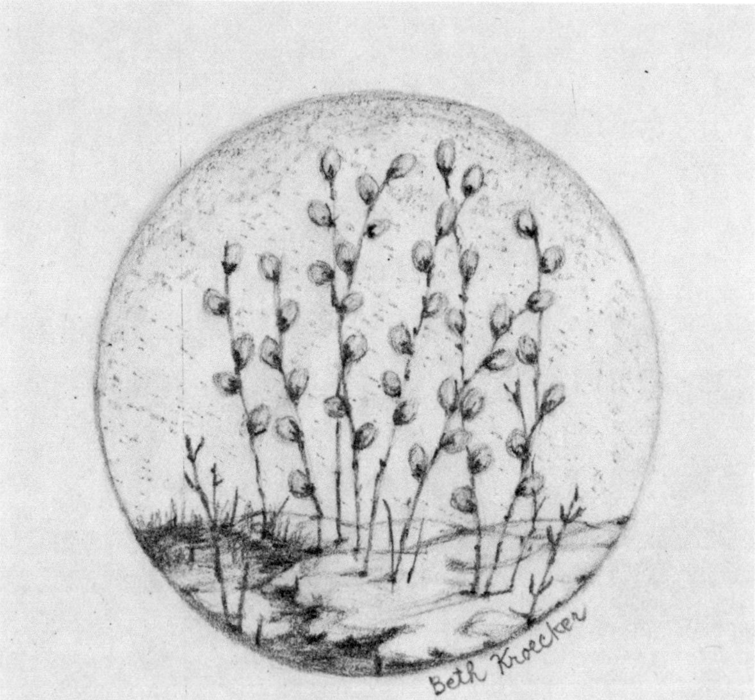
Beth Kroecker

Spring Planning

What a really
    Thoughtful thing;
To cover the buds
    With silken fur
As the willows
    Come forth
In the flurries
    Of spring.

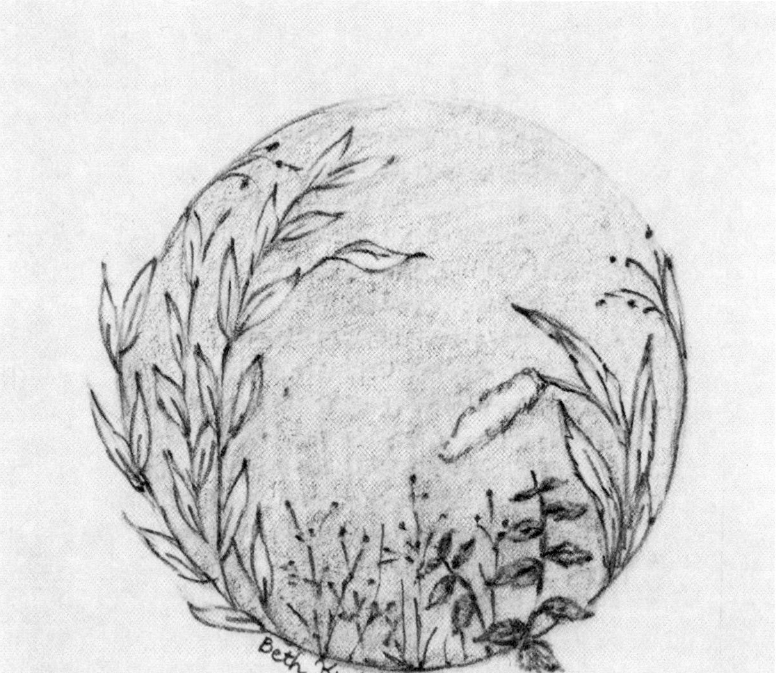
Beth Kroecken

Stille Stille

Breath of wind,
    Whisper
The willow's tress;
    Stille-stir
Sweet smells of
    Dark woods-earth,
Water grasses,
    Dew-mint sprigs,
New mown sod,
    And warm August sun
On spicy goldenrod.

Beth Kroecker

Storm

Today,
    Spring came
In a great
    Gust of
The gut;
    A pouring
Warm-storm;
    A cry,
Passionate welling
    Of all heaven
Throwing itself
    Upon the cold
Indifference of
    Frozen grime
And an old
    Winter time.

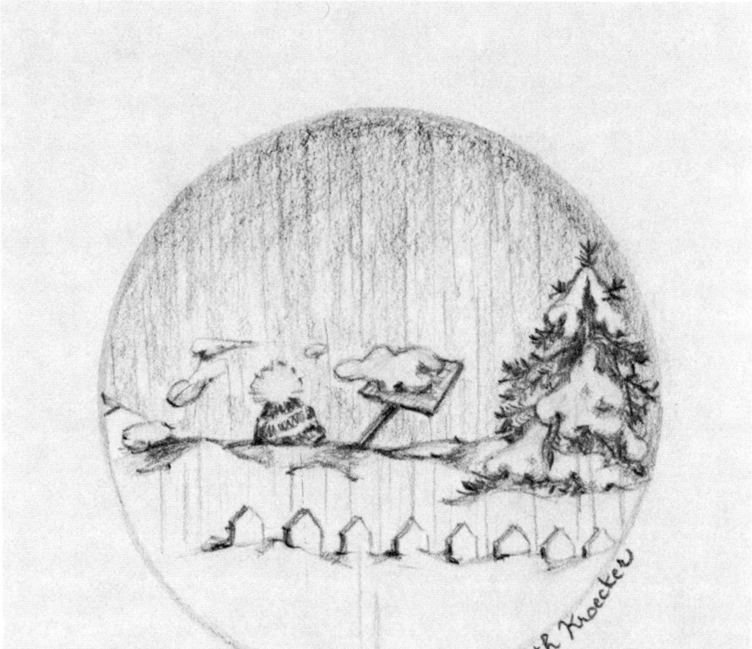
Beth Kroecker

Down Frown

Down
    Came the
Snow,
    Downer,
Downey,
    Downer;
I watched,
    A shovel
In my
    Hand
And a
    Frown
Upon my
    Face;
Frowner,
    Frowney,
Frowner.

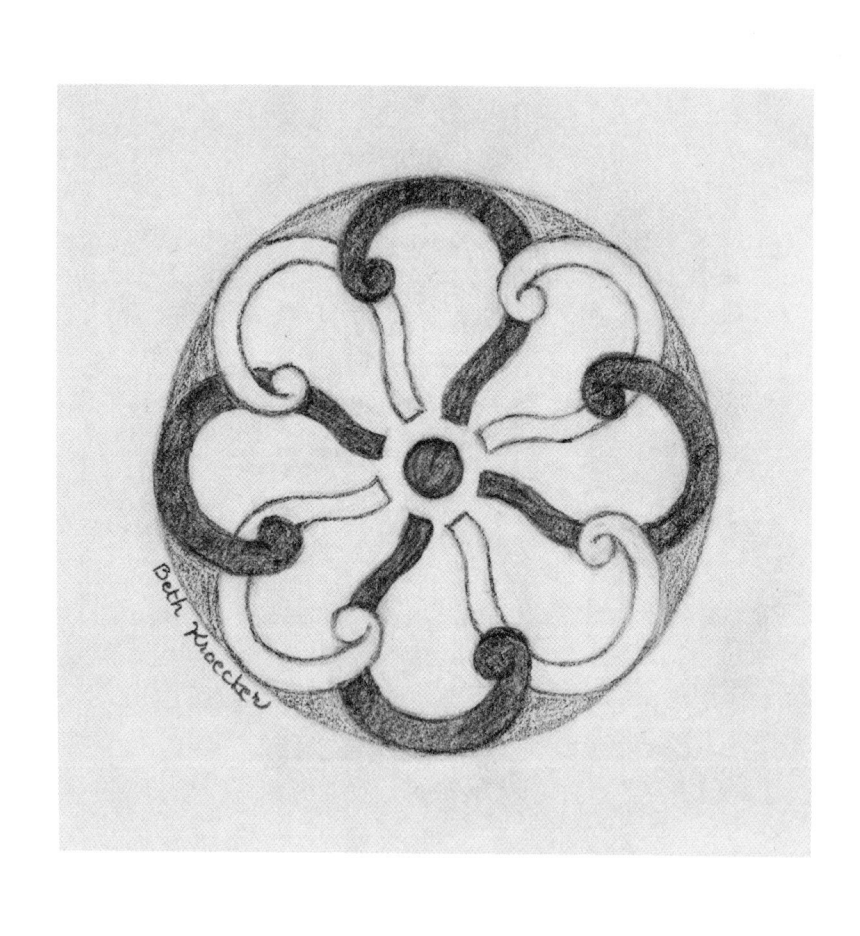
Beth Kroecker

Don't You Know?

What you
     Don't know,
You don't know;
     What you
Can't know,
     You won't.
What you
     Do know,
So often
     You don't.

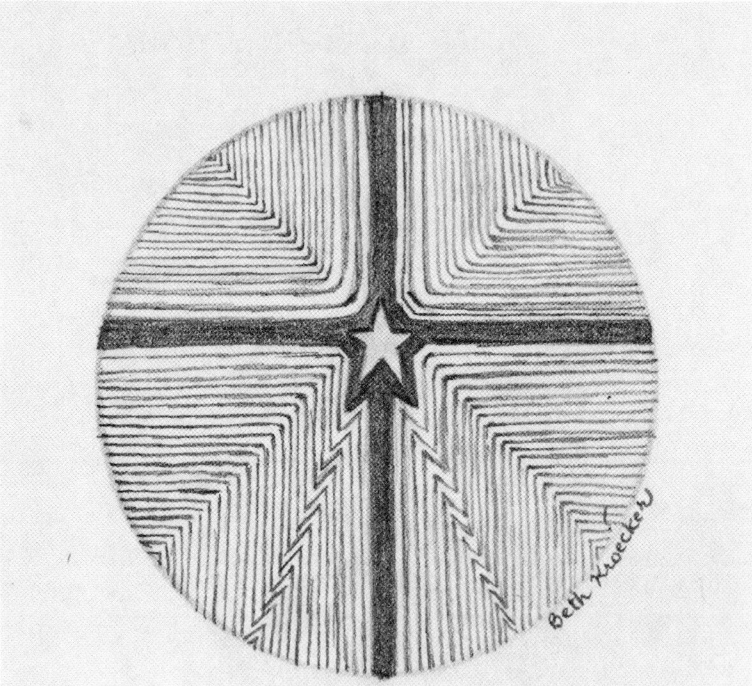
Beth Kroeker

Cover-Up

Did you ever notice,
    Dark of night,
The one you cannot see
    Is he who holds the light?

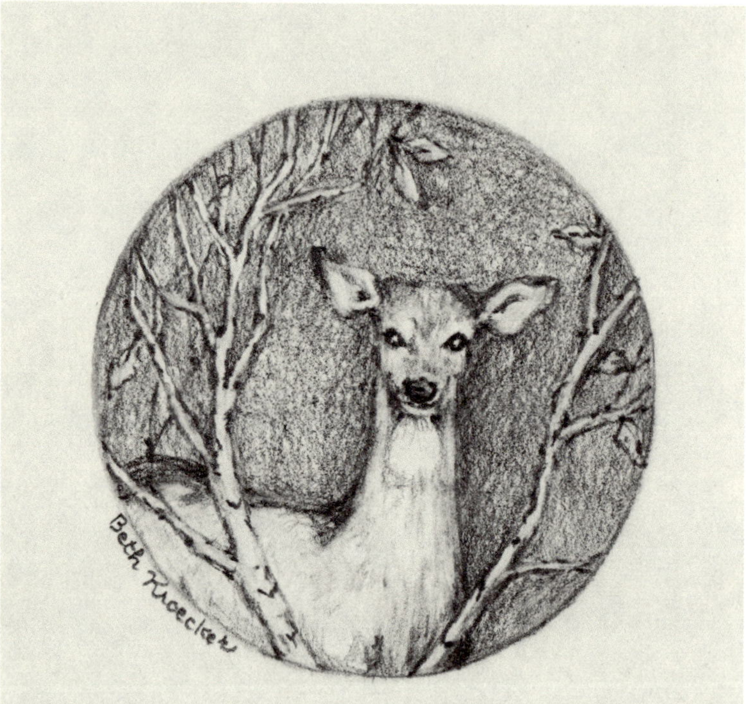
Beth Kroecker

Something In The Hunter

There's a fierce
Intelligence
    In a wild thing's
Eyes
    Bright knowings'
Incandescence
    When a wild thing
Dies;
    Hunters
Look away
    When a
Wild thing cries,
    And something
In the hunter
    Also dies.

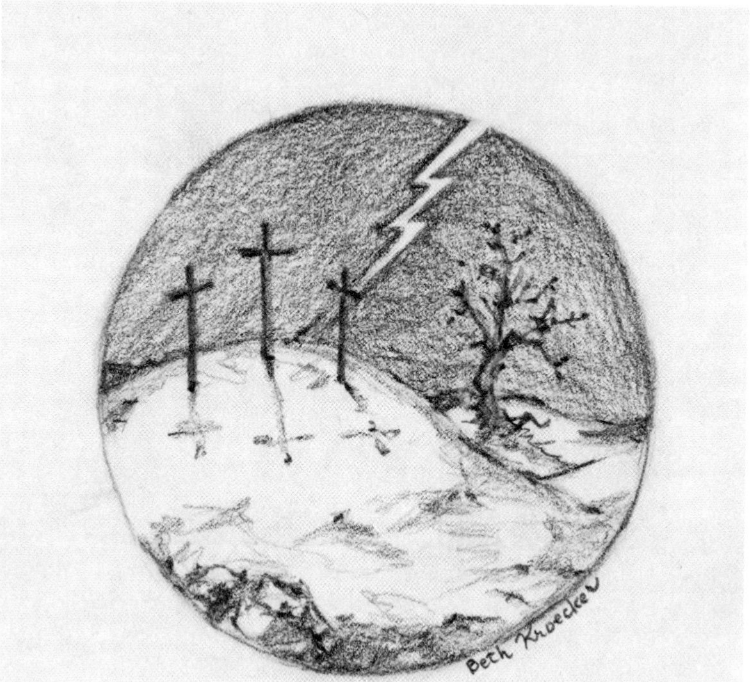
Beth Kroecker

Remorse

I will
    Ask you,
And you
    Reply
To me;
    Who
Suffered
    More --
Christ upon
    The cross,
Or Judas
    Walking
To his
    Tree?

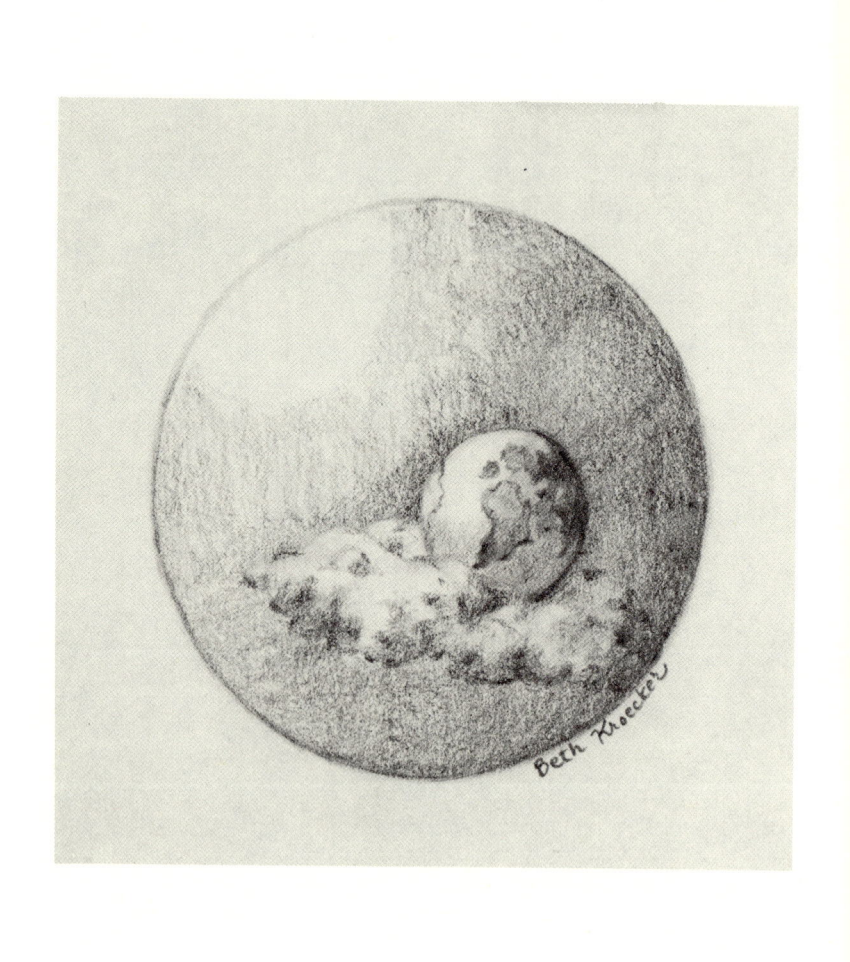
Beth Kroecker

Genesis

   Not me!
I wouldn't
  Make a cross;
I'd light a flame,
  Make a man,
Give him a name;
  I'll let you
Fashion the cross.

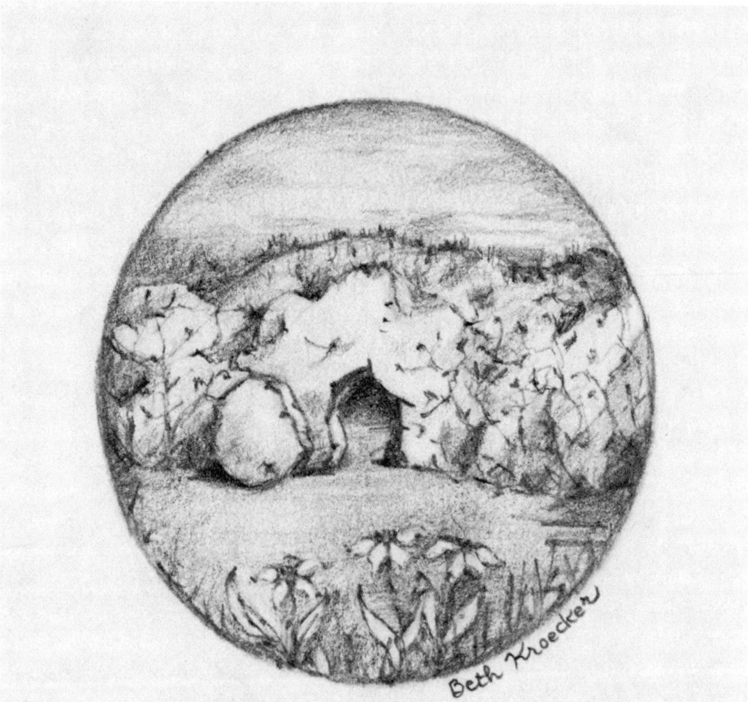
Beth Kroecker

In Extremis

Dying,
    Our prayers
Din heaven
    Appealing,
Forgetting
    That Death
Is the Final
    Healing

Beth Kroeker

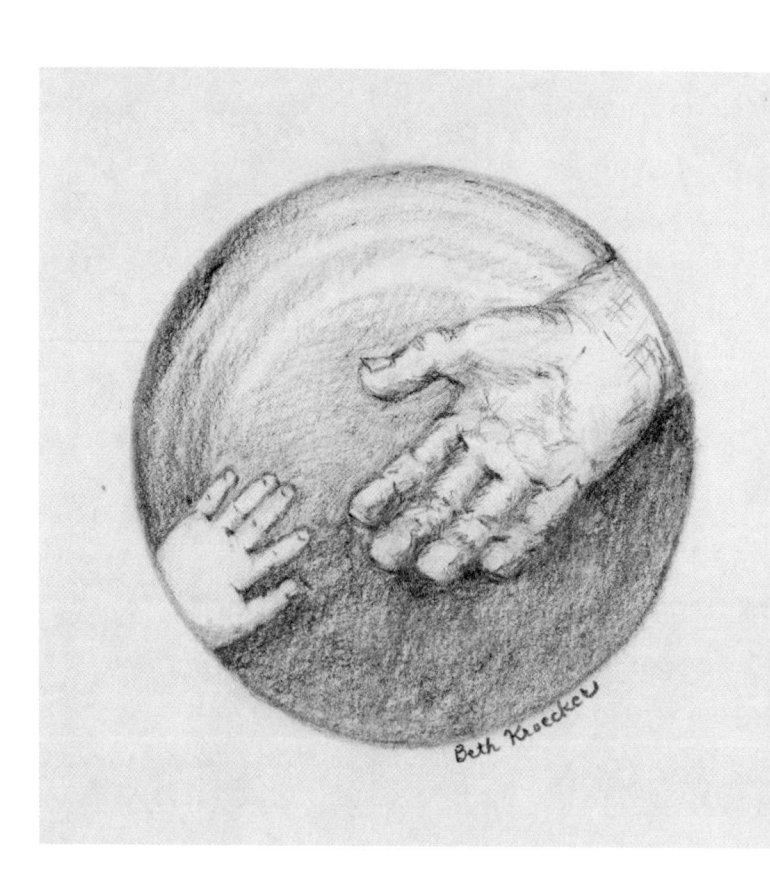

Empathy

May there be
    A rainbow
Between us--
    Between you
And me--
    May the sun
Shining
    Through our
Tears
    Be the
Ancient promise
    For all
The coming
    Years.

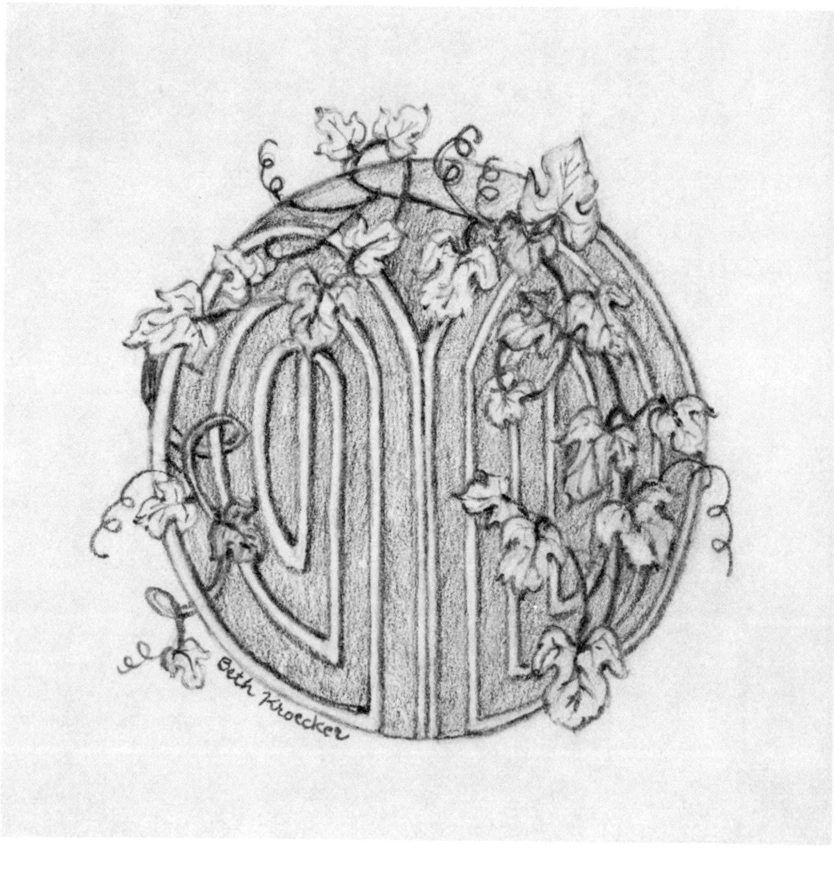
Beth Kroecker

Tough

I have no fears;
    Give me barbs
And guns
    And spears;
Conflicts and
    Battling hosts;
It's the
    "Gentle things"
That hurt
    The most.

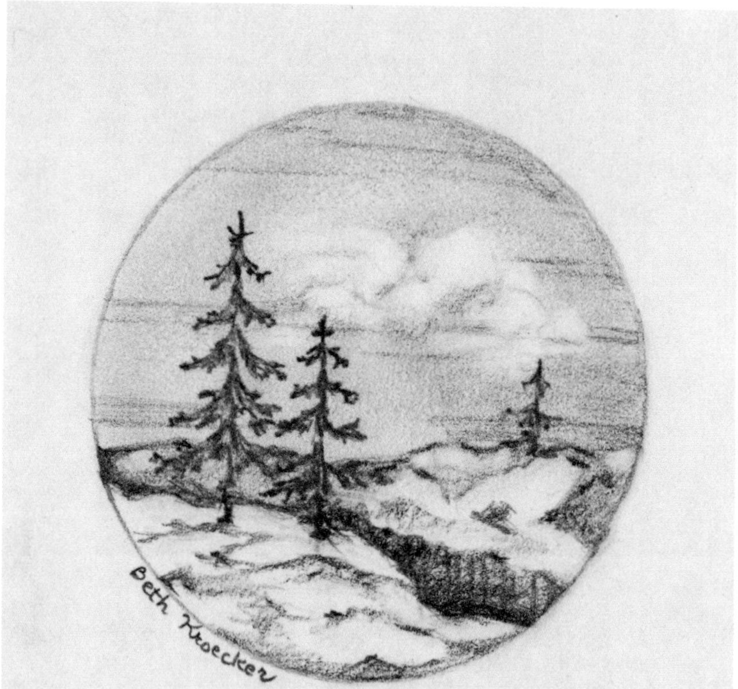
Beth Kroecker

Why Do I Know ?

I cannot fault the
    Beauty of the earth,
And I cannot understand
    How I should know
It is beauty.

I cannot explain
    The glory of the heavens,
And I cannot understand
    How I should know
It is glory.

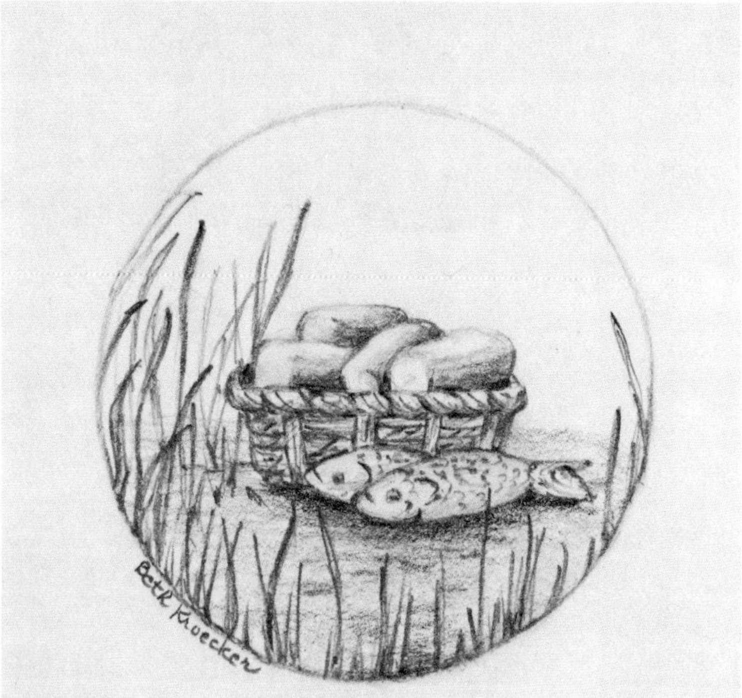
Beth Kroecker

Holy Grail

The miracle of the
Loaves and fishes
      was
Not so much
Bread and meat
      as
Love and wishes.

Not so much
Of mystery
      as
Hunger shared
      in
Chaliced hearts
      and
Common dishes.

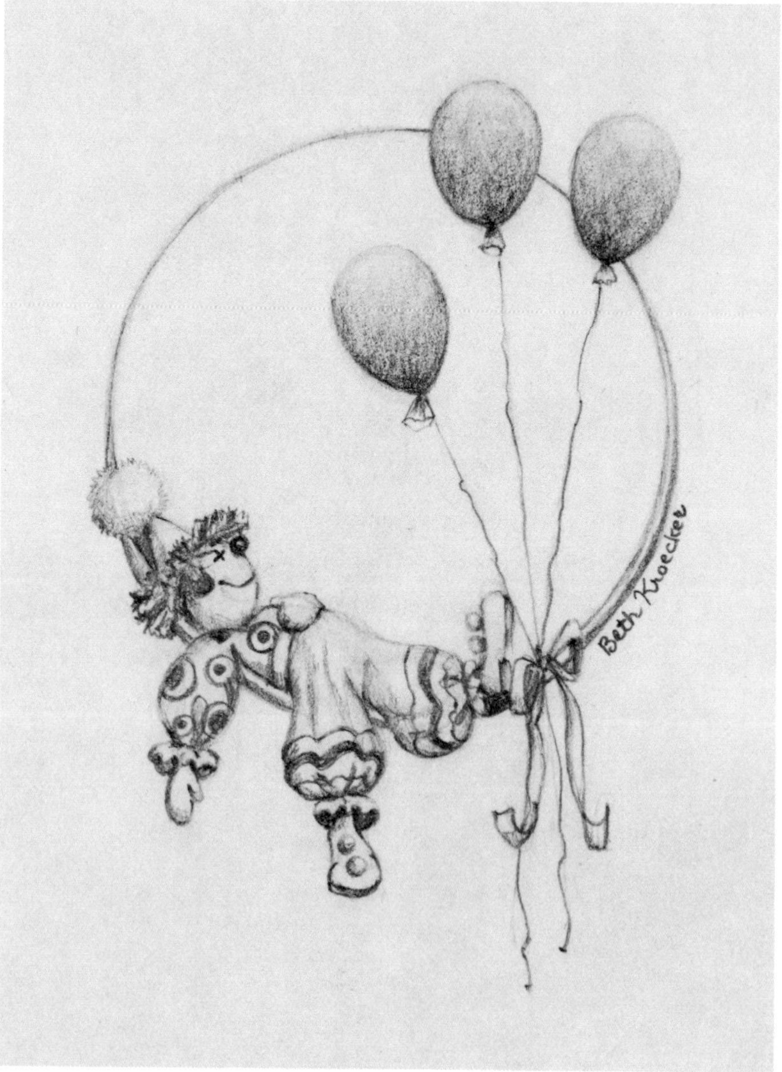
Beth Kroecker

Baby

Bethy
    Is whole,
She has
    Been given--
A laughing
    Soul.

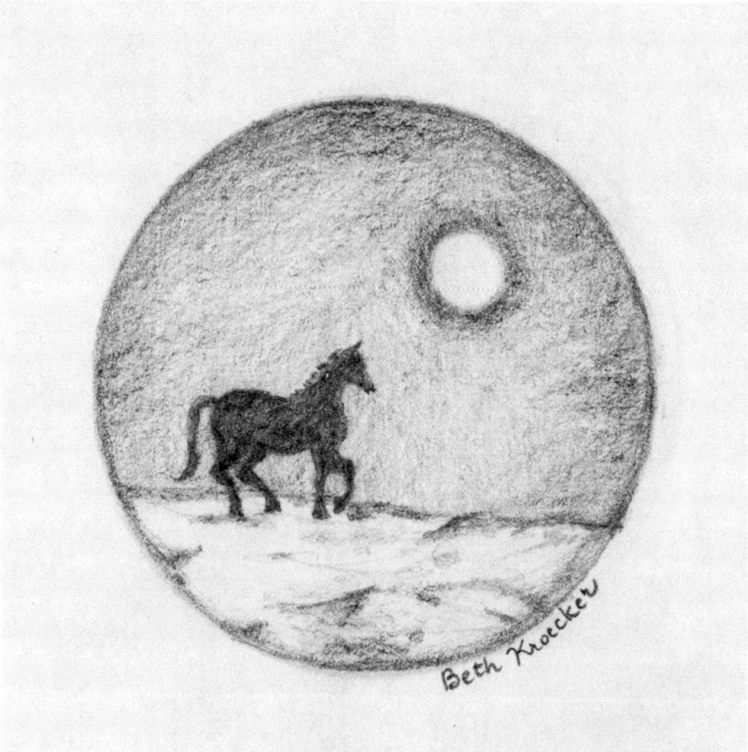
Beth Kroecker

22 - 80

In my time
    I have run
From horses
    To the moon
And all
    Too soon
Remembered
    I am
No more,
    No less,
Addled,
    No better,
Or smarter,
    For all the time
I've straddled.

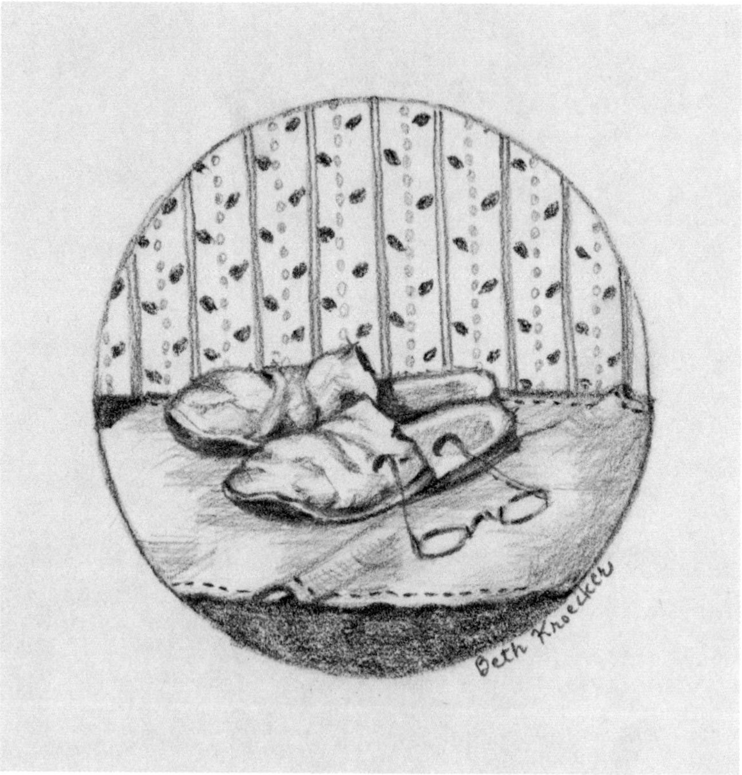
Beth Kroecker

It's Me

The pushers,
   Persuaders,
And pullers,
   Should know
That wrinkled skin
   Is soft,
Creased lips
   Are tender,
Gnarled hands
   Sensitive and feeling;
That faded eyes
   Can see
Both sides
   Of now;
It's not old-age
   It's me
Beneath this
   Wrinkled face,
Behind this
   Furrowed brow;
It's me.

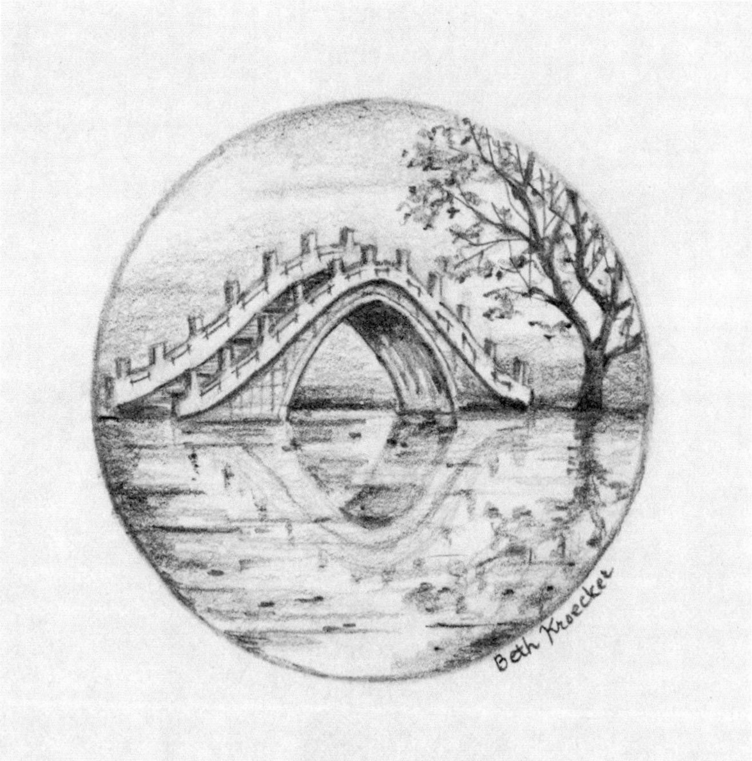
Beth Kroecker

Mooring Time

We are not the same;
    Time passed
Cannot be reclaimed;
    We are not where
We were;
    Awkward bridges
Are the words
    And worries
That tentatively
    Cast their lines
To moor.

Who?

Who made you
 Made you well;
It's important
 That you don't
Go to pieces.